Manifesting

Hidden Things The Law Of Attraction Revealed: The
Secret That No One Ever Told You About For Instant
Manifestation Miracles

*(The Complete Manifestation Guide For Drawing
Prosperity And Plenty Into Your Life)*

Nenad Lamprecht

TABLE OF CONTENT

Issue A Command That The Evil Mouth Be Shut 1

Activities That Involve Visualization 8

Figure Out How To Make Use Of The Name Of Jesus And The Power That He Gives You. 15

Your Ideal Way Of Life 25

Recognize And Overcome The Limiting Beliefs You Hold About Yourself 42

Always Attempt To Come Prepared 48

It Is More Vital To Have Imagination Than To Have Information. 57

Bringing Your Beliefs Into Line 66

Maintain Your Unwavering Belief 71

Encouraged Behavior 78

Love Yourself First In Order To Maintain Your Calm 86

Take What You Can From Your Past Mistakes, Then Get Back Up Again. 90

For The Sake Of Holy Guardianship 100

How To Make Things Happen More Quickly 111

Make The Decision To Put Your Happiness First. 116

Changes That Can Be Made 129

Creating A Spot For Parking Vehicles 139

Techniques Of Manifestation Utilizing Reiki 153

Liberation From Contemplations Of The Negative 159

Issue A Command That The Evil Mouth Be Shut

According to the Bible, Satan is referred to as "the accuser of the brethren."

After that, I heard a resounding voice in heaven proclaim, "Now have come the salvation, the power, and the kingdom of our God, and the authority of his Messiah." Because the one who brings charges against our brothers and sisters before our God at all hours of the day and night has been cast down...The Revealing

When the devil tempts someone to sin or causes someone to tempt God in the same way that he tempted Jesus when Jesus was brought into the wilderness by the Spirit of God, the devil then accuses that person. This is what the devil does.4-11 of the Gospel of Matthew. Because he warned him that "thou shalt not tempt the LORD your God," he is fully aware that your actions will provoke the wrath of the almighty. Matthew 4:1-7 (KJV)

He has a way of getting you to say things that go against God's will for you or comments that limit the power of God in your life; he can make you feel neglected and rejected by whispering a nasty word in your ear. He has a way of getting you to say things that go against God's will for you. Therefore, your petition is to compel the silencing of such a malicious voice, and to permanently close the hostile mouth that has been threatening your destiny.

Remember how Satan tricked Eve into believing that God does not want her to be like Him by telling her that God does not want her to be like Him. This caused Eve to sin against God, and as a direct result of Eve's transgression, she and her husband Adam lost the glory and the benefits that they had enjoyed in the Garden of Eden...origin of Things 3

INTERSECTIONS FOR PRAYER

a) Pray that your inner ear and heart are closed against the negative voices and thoughts b) Pray for positive thoughts and moves c) Pray for divine direction d) Pray for great opportunities that the opposing forces cannot stop e) Pray for disappointments of evil voice against your destiny a) Pray that your inner ear and heart are closed against the negative voices and thoughts b) Pray for positive thoughts and moves c) Pray for divine direction d) Pray for great opportunities

A DECLARATION AGAINST FORCES THAT LEAD TO A DELAY IN THE RECEIPT OF BLESSINGS

"However, the prince of the Persian realm put up a fight against me for a total of twenty-one days. When Michael, one of the chief princes, heard that I was being held there with the king of Persia, he came to my aid. Revelation 10:13

The plea of Daniel was heard, but the force of darkness that was acting in the second heavens, which the bible describes as principalities, held back the angel that was sent to bring the blessing to him, which caused the timing of him getting the benefit to be delayed. Daniel's prayer was answered.

You make the proclamation that God will save you from the evil forces that intend to work against your blessing in the new year of 2021 and that He will do so by delivering you from their grasp. In addition to this, they are to blame for preventing prayers from ascending to the third heaven, which is the location of God the Almighty. They will stop at nothing to accomplish that goal and give the appearance that God is not listening to or hearing people's prayers. They will sometimes shoot arrows that will make one's prayer weak, and in doing so, they will redirect some of the blessings that were going to come to that person to another person, most likely the person who honors and serves them. This practice is known as "manipulating the glory of another person."

In response to Daniel's fervent prayers, a higher authority within the angel was dispatched for the sake of Daniel to free the angel who was being held back.

I am aware of a person who is enduring severe financial hardship without receiving any assistance from any quarter. After suffering from disillusionment for such a long period of time, he eventually came to the conclusion that the only one who could help him was God, but the family and friends he had counted on to aid him deserted him. Following the completion of the prayer, anointing oil was then applied to him. During that week, he received a phone call from a helper who inquired about how they might assist him. It was very strange, considering that he had endured rejection and loneliness for a number of years, but all of a sudden, following prayer with anointing oil, he received a call of assistance during that week.

When the Lord opened my eyes to perceive this, I saw that his helper had already been released to him for years, but a force prevented the helper's connection with him. I also found out that his helper had been released to him. That is the effect that a network of such nefarious nature has on people.

PRAYER POINTS a) Pray against powers that cause delays in blessings. b) Pray also against powers that conceal or manipulate blessings. c) Pray that your blessings will not be for another person. d) Pray that you will always be in the right place at the right time. e) Pray for opened doors. f) Pray for showers of blessings. PRAYER POINTS a) Pray against powers that cause delays in blessings. b

Activities That Involve Visualization

Winners in every field employ a method called visualization to help them achieve their goals. Put your creative mind to work if you want something you've wished for so desperately to become a reality. Watch yourself accomplish what you desire, play the game in your head that you are about to play, or see the reward of your efforts already in front of you. Your own thoughts are the only thing holding you back.

Activities Available

You can establish new habits by using visualization, such as eating healthier foods or eating more slowly, which helps prevent overeating and obesity; have you ever seen an aerobatic airplane pilot imagining his or her routine on the ground using only their hands and their imagination? Have you ever simulated an interview with a potential employer in your head?

Imagine the desired activity, event, or outcome in your mind. Consider the idea that "what you see is what you get," and be prepared for imaginative thought and mental synthesis to take the initiative. If you want to build a train that runs on solar power, you should first picture such a train in your head, complete with shiny solar panels and a glistening exterior, and imagine it moving at a pace that you believe it would be able to achieve. Imagine anything, play it out in your head, and see it materialize before your eyes as images.

After spending a short amount of time, whether it be one minute, one day, one month, or even a significant amount of time, imagining the potential outcomes, you need now move to concentrate mode.

Concentrate intently on the mental image of the action you are about to carry out just at the very moment before you engage in the task, undertaking, or occurrence that will accomplish an outcome or even the outcome that will move you closer to achieving your goal.

For instance, if you're trying to hit a ball, visualize striking it in your head clearly stroke by stroke, at the appropriate height, and at the appropriate pace. This will help you hit the ball. Observe how the ball responds when it is struck by your instrument, how it travels through the air, and where it lands when it reaches its destination. Include all of your senses in the event; for example, you could hear the ball approaching, hear and feel the impact, and smell the grass. Then go ahead and do it seriously.

When you have a negative outlook on yourself and the opportunities available to you in life, nothing will get better. Nothing. A positive frame of mind can turn around a string of unlucky events. It will make what seemed like a glass half empty into a glass half full, and it will turn a cloudy day into a day with silver linings. Take use of the chances to improve yourself and keep going.

Anyone who expects change to take place overnight is setting themselves up for failure. If you don't look inward to find out what's wrong with you, you won't be any happier with your life in the next half year than you are right now, even if you win a fortune first thing in the morning.

Instead, you should establish a plan to bring your aspirations and dreams into reality over the long term.

Imagine where you will be in five, ten, and twenty years from now, along with the kinds of outcomes that you would like to see happen. Do not, on the other hand, simply take a snapshot of yourself in a flashy automobile, surrounded by a large mansion, a massive diamond collection, and pals who are groveling before you.

This is a superficial approach that, in the long term, will not be either healthy or gratifying. Instead, focus on the goals you want to achieve as a human being and the legacy you want to leave behind in both your community and the globe.

Visualization is only effective if you are relaxed, at ease, and prepared to give yourself the time and space to concentrate on it when you are undisturbed by your concerns. Visualization is a practice that is quite similar to meditation; yet, it is more dynamic and detailed than meditation.

You are urged to think actively about the possibilities when you are engaging in visualization; nevertheless, just like when you are meditating, you must put anything that is unrelated to your ambitions and objectives to the side and just concentrate on those.

Simply harboring the ambition to hold the presidency is not enough. You need to give some thought to the characteristics that will be beneficial to you in achieving this objective. Imagine not only winning the president but also having the qualities of being able to openly communicate, being strong, smiling, sharing, listening, talking, being able to deflect criticism with tact and respect, and other such qualities as well. There is a good chance that there will be talents that you need to improve, but like before, you can use visualization to zero in on certain skills and bring them up to par.

Figure Out How To Make Use Of The Name Of Jesus And The Power That He Gives You.

     Beloved, the most priceless inheritance that has been bestowed upon us is the glorious name of the Lord Jesus Christ. This was given to us as a gift. This is the most illustrious title that has ever been bestowed to a living human person. According to the Bible, God the Father bestowed this mighty name upon Jesus Christ, who is known as the Lord, before the foundation of the world. The power of the name of the Lord Jesus Christ is active in all three of these realms: heaven, earth, and the world beneath the earth. I would want to talk about the name of Jesus and how the early church and the apostles utilized this great name. They believed that everything that the Lord Jesus Christ accomplished throughout the time of his ministry on earth is accessible through the use of the name of the Lord Jesus

Christ. I would like to talk about how this wonderful name was used. Invoking the Holy Name of Jesus makes it possible to access everything that he learned and accomplished while he was tormented in hell, as well as the victory and the trophies that he gained in the open conflict that he fought against the adversary. This name is necessary for us, and we may use it to connect to the master and make use of his resources and abilities in the same manner that they would have been available to him in his own life.

Matthew 28:18 should be read. After that, Jesus came up to them and declared, "All authority in heaven and on earth has been given to me." 19 Therefore, as you go, make disciples of people from all nations by baptizing them in the name of the Father, the Son, and the Holy Spirit, and teach them to obey all that the Father has commanded you. Acts 2 verse 38 Peter responded to them by saying, "In order to have your sins forgiven, each one of you must turn away from your sins and be baptized in the name of Jesus Christ, the Messiah. After that, the gift of the Holy Spirit will be bestowed upon you. (International Standard Version) This is the location where the Lord Jesus Christ gave his followers the official instruction to preach the word of God in his name. The original disciples were given the directive to baptize any new converts in the name of the Holy Trinity: the Father, the Son, and the Holy Spirit. It was at this point that people began to invoke the name of Jesus Christ in their conversations. The next thing that you need to know about this instruction is that in order to make use of all of the powers that are found in Christ Jesus, you need to call upon the magnificent name. The Lord Jesus Christ possesses all power and authority because it was bestowed upon him by the Father, but the only method for us to access and exercise that power and authority is via the name of the Lord Jesus Christ.

1 John 3: 23 And this is the commandment he gave us: that we should believe in the name of his Son, Jesus the Messiah, and that we should love one another as he commanded us to do. (ISV)

10:9 from Romans You will be saved if you confess with your mouth that Jesus Christ is Lord and believe in your heart that God resurrected him from the dead. This is the only way to receive salvation. 10 Because one must believe in his heart in order to be vindicated, and one must declare with his mouth in order to be rescued. (ISV) The great apostle of the Lord Jesus Christ, who also received a great deal of insight and inspiration from both the Lord and the Father, is writing to believers in the Lord as well as new converts in order to remind them about the essential tenets of their faith. He stated that Jesus Christ, Lord is the Messiah, and that it is God's will for all people in the world to believe in the name of Jesus Christ, Lord. This is the will of God for the world. In the name of the Lord, we are also being charged with the obligation to love one another. Can you see that, in the name of Jesus, we believe in the accomplished work of Christ, and in the name of Jesus, we are commanded to love one another?

John 20:31 should be read. But these things have been written down for you so that you may believe that Jesus is the Messiah, the Son of God, and so that you may have life in his name as a direct result of your belief in him. (In the International Standard Bible Version) Beloved, the word of God admonishes us to the fact that if we trust in the name of Jesus, we will be granted eternal life. This adds yet another facet to the multifaceted nature of the use of the name Jesus. According to the teachings of the Bible, all that is required of us to be eligible for the gift of eternal life is to have faith in the name of the Lord Jesus Christ.

Please read Acts 3:1-6. Peter, on the other hand, responded by saying, "I don't have any silver or gold, but I'll give you what I do have." Walk in the name of Jesus Christ, the Messiah who came from Nazareth! (ISV)

Hello there, this passage of scripture discusses the apostles' use of the extraordinary power that Jesus gave them in the name of Jesus. The backstory of the narrative focuses on the situation of a disabled guy who typically asks passersby for alms. As was his custom, when this man who was physically unable to function saw the disciples approaching the temple, he accosted them in order to beg for alms. However, in contrast to other people, the followers of Jesus were able to give this man who was disabled complete healing for his body. Apostle Peter told the guy that despite the fact that he did not possess any silver or gold, he would give the man whatever he possessed. The name of Jesus was the item in question that Peter possessed. Peter then ordered in the name of Jesus, the Messiah from Nazareth, and demanded that the man be well. Instantly, the man was healed, and he began walking in the temple. Here, the name is used to heal the man who was lame.

Please read Acts 3:16. This individual, who you see and are familiar with, was made well as a result of having trust in his name, which is why his name is important. Indeed, he owes his flawless health here and now in front of all of you to the faith that is found in Jesus. (ISV)

Read Acts 4:10; in the International Standard Version of the Bible, this passage states that "you and all the people of Israel must understand that this man stands healthy before you because of the name of Jesus from Nazareth, whom you crucified, but whom God raised from the dead."

These two passages of scripture are also drawn from the anecdotes of persons who got healing at the hands of the Lord. In point of fact, the Bible states that the disciples of Jesus spread the word of their master throughout Jerusalem. However, that was not all that they did; the Bible also states that they carefully followed their master's instructions, and in His name, they cured a wide variety of illnesses. To the glory of God, the Apostles accomplished a variety of strong and miraculous works, including resurrecting the dead and healing the sick. If you wish to operate at the same level as these disciples did, then you need to master the principles that guided their outstanding performance in the work that God gave them to do. The answer can be found in the name of the Christ, who is the Lord. If you employ it in the fight against diseases, sicknesses, paralysis, and death, you will emerge victorious.

11th verse of 1 Corinthians That's what some of you were doing, wasn't it? But in the name of our Lord Jesus Christ, the Messiah, and by the Holy Spirit of our

God, you have been cleansed, you have been sanctified, and you have been justified. (In the International Standard Version) This should serve as a reminder to the believer that our sanctification and justification were all accomplished in the name of the Lord Jesus Christ. These wondrous works, which were performed on us to the glory of the Almighty God, were carried out by the Holy Spirit. Because we have put our faith in the name of Jesus, the Holy Spirit has set us apart from sinful people, sanctified us, and given us justification in the eyes of God as righteous individuals. As a result, we can now call ourselves legitimate children of God.

You will continually give thanks to God the Father for everything in the name of our Lord Jesus Christ, who is the Messiah; (Ephesians 5:20, International Standard Version).

Since I have already written a sufficient amount on this subject, you should now be aware that the early church carried out practically all of its activities in the name of the Lord Jesus Christ. This biblical passage is drawing attention to the fact that even the act of expressing gratitude was performed in the name of the Lord Jesus Christ. My understanding is that learning to perform actions in the name of the Lord Jesus Christ is the most effective approach to win the approval of the heavenly Father. If you start from someplace and do it deliberately, you will be amazed by the growth and fruitfulness that will rock both your life and your ministry.

Your Ideal Way Of Life

If all you had to do was wish for anything, and your wish would come true, wouldn't you hope for the best life possible? Certainly you would, and so would the rest of us if only it were that simple. The most challenging aspect would be imagining what your ideal existence would be like in its entirety and working backwards from there. Because we have no means of knowing exactly what our future is going to look like nor how much time we have to make that future a reality, it is simple to be general about the things that we hope for the future.

If we are genuinely present in the moment and our primary focus is meeting the requirements of the circumstance in which we find ourselves, then figuring out what it is that we require will be a lot less difficult. Therefore, when you first start using the talent of manifesting, it is likely that you will be concentrating on the needs and desires that you currently have. There is absolutely no problem with it, and it appears to be the choice that is most consistent with logic while also being extremely in tune with human nature. What happens, then, when all of your immediate requirements are satisfied and you begin daydreaming about achieving everything you've ever desired in your life?

where you get to this point, difficulties can start to arise, and this is also the point where the universe might decide to give you a good shake and force you to examine your logic a bit more carefully. Permit me to illustrate with an example: Let's say you've always dreamed of owning a large and luxurious boat. Are you able to swim? Do you have motion sickness on the boat? Are you able to pay for the upkeep, the dock fees, the storage, the gasoline, and the insurance on your boat? Do you have experience operating a large boat? Do you make your home near the water? Do you have a working knowledge of nautical flags, maps, and the various types of warning flares? How thoroughly have you mulled over the concept of what it actually means to own something of this sort and how it can affect your life? If you go around begging the universe to deliver this massive vessel to your doorstep, ask yourself if you are truly going to be prepared for all of the difficulties that come along with it. Possibly, you are prepared, and if this is the case, the universe will be more than glad to grant you the wish of your heart. Will it bring you contentment and tranquility in the long run, and what do you plan to do after that?

People have the tendency to believe that they know what they want until they actually receive it, at which point they realize that they are not prepared to deal with what it is that they have obtained. Sometimes the universe has a dark sense of humor and chooses to teach us lessons the hard way so that we might avoid making the same mistakes in the future. However, the majority of the time, the universe is not going to let that happen. We are all capable of behaving like children at times, and the universe will respond to our antics like a loving parent by caving in to our demands in order to provide us the opportunity to discover life's lessons on our own. It is the truly smart man (or woman) who is aware of their limitations and seeks advice before they make a fool of themselves, rather than allowing themselves to be made a fool of and then seeking assistance in order to fix an issue that they themselves have brought into existence.

Manifesting is a straightforward process that still yields powerful results. You are doing more than letting fate to run your life when you put your desire out there into the cosmos and then let the universe do what it will with that request. You are accepting that you are aware that you do not have the power and talents to control every single aspect of your life. There are a lot of people who can't or won't just let life happen to them like that. Manifesting is not the same as sitting in a daze all day and expecting the cosmos to run your life for you while you do nothing but stare into space. The process of manifesting is a two-way street, and you have a part to play in it. The things in your life that are under your control that you can accomplish for yourself are your duty. The things that you can't get for yourself are the things that you're able to bring into existence. Even so, the universe anticipates that you will take an active part in the maintenance of all of the aspects of your life that are under your control. Manifesting is not about gaining things as status symbols; rather, it is about having the means to live your life in a manner that magnifies the power of the universe and offers peace and happiness to those who are in need. Manifesting is about having the means to live your life in a manner that magnifies the power of the universe. Nevertheless, manifesting is not the same thing as having to live in abject poverty. To a greater extent, manifestation is about learning to make do with what you have while maintaining a state of oneness with the cosmos. Respecting what you already have, what nature offers, what may come your way, what others have, and what may happen to all the people and things around you at any one time is an important part of the practice of manifesting.

The practice of manifesting has the potential to alter your life in ways that you are unable to even begin to fathom at this point. A seemingly insignificant shift in your life right now may have significant and unforeseeable repercussions for your future. If you take the time today to allow the universe to function in your life, it is possible that a seemingly insignificant alteration may turn into a significant shift in your way of living, or that it will introduce you to other individuals who will play a significant role in the development of your future. There is no way to know what the universe has in store for you at any particular instant in time since there is no way to forecast it. You have the opportunity to slow down, ask for your current needs and goals, and open the door for future changes if you are prepared to allow your oneness to expand via the process of manifesting. Manifesting gives you this opportunity. You can't just ask for something once or twice and then ignore it until you need something else, at which point you may start asking again. Incorrect; in order to manifest, you must first cultivate and strengthen your connection to the oneness, as well as spend time in a state of mental stillness and calm, so that miraculous occurrences may take place not only in response to your specific requests but all the time.

When I give presentations about manifesting, the number one criticism I hear from attendees is that they do not have enough time. When we have time to watch television, text our friends, surf the internet, and engage in a wide variety of other activities that squander time, I find it very difficult to accept that. If you sincerely want to make your life better, you will make time, even if it is just a small amount, to begin the process of developing a sense of oneness with the source that was responsible for your creation and that continues to keep watch over your life every day. When you first begin your investigation into the world of oneness, the best times to do so are very early in the morning or very late in the evening. When you first wake up, the outside world has not yet had a chance to attach itself to your brain and fill all of the empty spaces with the noise and confusion of everyday life. Everyone needs some time to themselves in the evening to wind down and recharge after the challenges they faced during the day. These two time spans are ideal for contemplating what it is you need to do to make your life more useful not only to yourself but to the universe as a whole, as well as for praying to the universe for the strength to deal with the challenges of life and asking for its assistance in doing so.

When you have made the practice of emptying your mind a habit and when you discover that you can incorporate it into your life more frequently, you will find that you are able to send a request floating out into the cosmos at any given point in time as if it were second nature to you. The process of manifestation will grow more haphazard and require less thought, and you won't understand what you've accomplished until you see the results of your efforts. You will want to tell everyone you meet about this amazing new information that you have acquired, and some people will pay attention to what you have to say, while others will consider you to be completely insane.

Wouldn't it be wonderful if everyone gave manifestation a shot, learnt about its advantages, discovered their own inner peace, and the world as a whole became a kinder, gentler, and more peaceful place to live? Manifesting can be defined as the process of bringing one's desires into physical form. We can keep harboring the belief that this will come to pass, just as a great number of influential people in the past have done. Many examples of people throughout history who used manifesting or a technique quite similar to it, but people still refused to listen to them may be found in historical records. Why is it that the world ignores something that is so amazing even when it is brought to their attention? Because the seed of uncertainty has been put in our minds ever since the beginning of time. We have the power to overcome that skepticism and bring about change not only in our own lives but also in the world's overall trajectory. Sadly, the world is not yet prepared to listen; the word "yet" is important here. There may come a day when people are ready to give up greed, wars, pride, debt, hatred, and a whole host of other ills, but until that day comes, there will only be a select few that comprehend a simple idea and use it to improve both their own lives and the environment around them that they can manage. Until that day comes, there will only be a select few that grasp a simple principle and use it to improve both their own lives and the environment around them that they can control.

The act of manifesting has the potential to alter not only your life but also your planet, your mentality, and your future. It does not follow that the life that you consider to be your dream life right now will be the same life that you consider to be your dream life twenty years from now. It has been established beyond a reasonable doubt that as we become older, the characteristics of our ideal existence shift with time. That does not mean, however, that you cannot attain what it is that you actually want if doing so is truly feasible given the resources at your disposal. You cannot, however, bring into physical existence something that is not even remotely possible. If you've never taken even a single medical class in your entire life, you won't be able to sleep tonight thinking you're going to wake up tomorrow with the title of world's finest neurosurgeon. On the other hand, an offer from a medical school could come to you in the mail. In the event that you require the services of the most qualified neurosurgeon, your oneness connection with the world will find a method to put you in contact with the appropriate individual. Once we have developed this connection with the universe (even though we have actually always been connected and simply didn't know it), there is a unique capacity to be able to reach out and touch someone without even recognizing that we have done so. This is because we are all connected, and once we have developed this connection with the universe, there is a unique ability to be able to touch someone without even realizing that we have done so. It is also believed that if your oneness is strong enough, you ought to be able to make direct contact as easily as dialing a phone number provided that your oneness is sufficiently strong. If the universe is willing to allow us to have this power, then I don't see any reason why we should stand in their way. It's possible that there are certain individuals with whom I do not wish to have such a connection; on the other hand, it would be wonderful to be able to speak in this manner with such individuals if they had similar perspectives.

It is thought that a person who has developed a strong connection to the concept of oneness has the power to walk on air, hot coals, or even water. You've probably been told accounts of something like this taking place at some point in the past. We should be able to ignore the concept of gravity and truly float free from the surface of the Earth since there is no concept of time anywhere in the cosmos. If this is the case, then we should be able to float. Again, if the universe is going to allow it to happen, then it should be so. This is not something that every person would be able to develop, but if the universe is going to allow it to happen, then it should.

When people have attained a level of oneness, there have been reported incidents of their going into what looks to be a trance and having a lowered heartbeat and breathing rate. These people also have had their heartbeat and breathing rate slow down. Again, because there is no predetermined time constraint to adhere to, these human characteristics are not required for journeying around the universe with your higher power. They are still breathing and their hearts are still beating, even though it is obvious that without fundamental human functions, their bodies would not be able to continue living. It never ceases to astonish medical professionals how the human body can continue to function so normally despite being subjected to such harsh conditions without exhibiting any symptoms of harmful effects.

Obviously, achieving the level of oneness that allowed a person to accomplish such remarkable things would need a life filled with a great deal of devotion at every turn. It's possible that some people would like to change their lives to that extent, but the majority of people desire to better their current life without drawing additional attention to it. This is comprehensible and is most likely what the one who created us anticipates from us. It does not imply that we should disregard the pull of the will of the power source of the cosmos; rather, it suggests that we ought to have a tremendous degree of respect for what might be.

Every day, there are millions of people all around the world whose requirements and preferences are being communicated in one way or another. Each cry is heard by the universe, and it reacts in its own unique way. Sometimes we fail to see the whole grand scheme of the entire cosmos, which leads to our unrealistic expectations of instant outcomes. What can appear to be a straightforward request to us might in fact be connected to the requests of other people, and the universe will figure out a way to make sure that everyone's wants are addressed in some way. Can you picture yourself working in that field? Humans are a needy and demanding bunch and sometimes we have to learn to laugh at ourselves. There is a good chance that the universe spends a good deal of its time laughing at humans. We appear to be so certain that we know exactly what we require until we receive it, at which point we begin to grumble that it is not adequate or that we desired something more suitable. Sometimes the cosmos is aware of this, and because it knows us so well, it provides us with something better as a reward.

You can spend some time planning on how you think you might achieve the life of your dreams, what steps you need to start taking now, and start making those manifest requests to the powers of the universe and see what begins to happen while you're trying to figure out what your dream life should be and how that is going to fit into the grand scheme of the plans the universe has. This can be done while you're trying to determine what your dream life should be and how that is going to fit into the grand scheme of the plans the universe has.

Recognize And Overcome The Limiting Beliefs You Hold About Yourself

When you are writing about your desire, you should make sure that you put down any limiting belief that comes into your thoughts during the process. Every one of us is held back from moving forward by limiting beliefs that act as shackles on our minds and prevent us from progressing. Your limiting beliefs include thoughts such as "What if I fail? ", "I don't have the skill to do so," "I will never succeed," "I don't have the talent," and others of a similar nature, and their sole purpose is to prevent you from growing as an individual.

Discovering all of these limiting beliefs will help you understand the thoughts and beliefs that need to be changed in order for you to become unstoppable. Record every belief, and then conduct an in-depth examination of each one.

Consider the origin of each belief, and if it is one that was taught to you by someone else, investigate the veracity of that teacher's statements. If, for example, someone referred to you as a failure, what evidence do you have to validate their statement? If there is no evidence to support the claim, go on to the next concern. If you discover that a limiting thought you hold is founded on your own anxiety, you should investigate the veracity of the belief and hunt for evidence to disprove it. For instance, if you believe that your lack of sufficient abilities inhibits your advancement, why don't you put some effort into developing those skills?

Consider the several approaches you could take to conquer the insecurities and phobias that, in some way, gave rise to your limiting beliefs. Doing so will allow you to rid yourself of negative beliefs and foster more constructive ones.

At the same time, you need to begin having encouraging and kind conversations with yourself in your head. You should accept a limiting thought whenever it appears in your head, but you should also replace it with something that is geared toward your development. alter your thinking to "Of course, I can become a millionaire if I work hard and believe in my power and the LOA." If you previously thought, "I can never become a millionaire," alter it to "Of course, I can become a millionaire." To ensure that your idea is easily believed, you should strive to make it as realistic as possible. You have to make it a habit to talk favorably to yourself so that you always give yourself positive recommendations and convert limiting beliefs into growth oriented ones. If you do this, you will be able to change limiting beliefs into growth oriented ones.

It is one thing to have ambitious goals and another to actually work toward achieving those goals. In order to realize any ambitious goal, you will first need to break it down into more manageable chunks and establish a series of milestones along the way. This will make the task less daunting. After you have finished daydreaming and are confident that you know what your ultimate, end objective is, break it down into tiny parts and pieces so that you can work on goals that are more manageable.

Have faith in both the Cosmos and the process.

After that, you must have faith that the universe and the Law of Attraction as a whole will guide you to the place you see for yourself. You have to have an optimistic expectation about your objective and every day of your life with absolute certainty, and you have to be convinced that you have placed your destiny in the hands of a power that is far greater and more powerful than your own. The more faith you have in its efficacy, the more rapidly you will accomplish what you set out to do.

Stop questioning the power of the cosmos and whether or not you will actually be able to tap into it if you want to believe in its potential. Throw out any thoughts that begin with "if" or "but" and replace them with steadfast convictions whenever they enter your mind. In order to effectively tap into the power of the cosmos, you will need to provide it with more than just a singular objective. You need to put in writing not just what it is that you want but also what it is that you are willing to give up in order to get it. Sincerity and honesty are the only two qualities that can build trust, and in order to earn someone's trust, you have to be honest about what you want and how you plan to get it.

What are you planning to do to trade your time for a monthly income of $20,000? That's the question I'm asking since I'm interested in hearing your answer. Consider your abilities and the potentials you possess, and how you may put those to use in order to accomplish your goal. If you are a copywriter, you may do that to get your desired income, or if you are a realtor, perhaps that is how you aim to make $50,000 per month in commissions. Put your plans to reach your objective in writing and include a description of how you want to get there. It may be something like, "Starting in October 2019, I am going to earn $50,000 each month working as a realtor to the best of my abilities." if you want to give an example.

When you share with the universe exactly what it is that you want and how you plan to get it, you are demonstrating that you are willing to trust it with the most private details of your life, and this allows you to gradually begin to develop faith in the process.

You need to make use of two key LOA tools, which we will go over in the following , in order to go closer and closer to achieving your objective.

Always Attempt To Come Prepared

Although it is the slogan of the Boy Scouts, it is also going to be something that you will want to live your life by. A winner is always ready for anything may come their way. They make certain that they are prepared for whatever they have planned by ensuring that they have all that is necessary for their success. That implies that regardless matter whether they are organizing a backyard barbecue or the launch of a new firm, they always know what they are doing and they always have anything they may need to be entirely successful in whatever endeavor they are undertaking. The question now is, what can you do to ensure that you are always ready?

Make certain that you are well-versed in the topic at hand before proceeding to the next step. This is the most important step. Make sure you have a clear idea of what you want the end result to be. Decide if you want to have a pizza party or a barbecue if you're throwing a party for your pals at your house, for instance. The dynamic will shift slightly as a result of the various types of gatherings that take place. After all, if you want to have a pizza party, you'll need pizza, and if you want to have a barbecue, you'll need food that can be cooked on a grill. If you throw many different kinds of parties or organize several different kinds of events, you might invite various people each time.

Once you have a clear understanding of what your idea is, the next step is to comprehend what the actual strategy entails. When folks arrive at the location, or when you've put your initial plan into motion, what are you going to do next? You need to make sure that you are ready for anything that may come your way, and that includes being aware of what steps to take both if things go according to plan and if they do not.

Therefore, consider what it is that you would require if everything were to run smoothly. It's possible that you'd like to give a presentation to your manager. What steps would you take next if they indicated that they enjoyed the way everything got started? Create a plan that encompasses the entire process, from the very beginning to the very end, and ensure that everything follows it to the letter.

Now it's time to start thinking about what could possibly go wrong. A winner never loses sight of the opportunities that lie before them and never stops looking for methods to improve their situation. If you are ready for the absolute worst that could happen, then you will be able to prevent a problem from becoming a major issue before it even starts. Instead of being trapped on a road that leads to disaster, you will have the ability to turn everything around in the direction that you want it to go.

Do you remember when you were in school and you were required to write so many essays? Your introduction was always going to be in the first paragraph. At that point, you stated what you were going to talk about as well as the reasons why what you were going to talk about was such an essential subject. You provided an overview of your argument as well as the reasons why people should agree with you. But in the second paragraph, you completely reversed the order of things. You centered your attention in the second paragraph on the most significant critique leveled against your plan and idea, and you provided an explanation of why either the criticism leveled against your plan was not truly valid at all or why your idea was not a good one.

When preparing anything, the most crucial thing to do is to think about what objections or problems could possibly arise from the plan. When you have that information, you will be able to make preparations for it, and you will have a better idea of what steps you need to do in order to put things right. Take, for instance, the fact that you are organizing a barbecue. You will have a delicious supper, and you will have fun spending time with your friends if everything goes according to plan. It's possible that you might even spend some time conversing or playing games. You may get to know someone new, or you could simply rekindle old friendships with someone you haven't talked to in a while, which would allow you to relax and take your mind off of things for a time.

What if it ends up raining? Even though you won't be able to enjoy a barbecue in the fresh air if it's raining, it doesn't mean you can't still have a wonderful time. What plans do you have if it starts raining? What would happen if you prepared the meal inside the house but continued to host your guests anyway?

You've successfully averted at least one potential disaster with your actions. You are now prepared for the possibility that it will rain. What are some more challenges that could possibly arise? Perhaps one of your closest pals is obligated to go to work today. As a result, they won't be able to visit us. Do I have it right that you'll still be able to have other folks over? You will not be prevented from having a wonderful time. Another potential catastrophe has been averted.

What you need to do is consider the various scenarios that could take place and then formulate a strategy for how you would proceed in each of those circumstances. Now, you don't want to go completely crazy with this. Someone who is successful is not someone who overthinks every situation. It is not necessary for you to spend time considering, for instance, what you would do in the event that a meteor smashed into the earth. Pay attention to the things that are genuinely quite likely and that you may really have to find a way to work around. These are the things that, rather than simply making you paranoid, will make you prepared for whatever may come your way.

Being prepared is a state of mind, the same as all of the other aspects that we have explored so far. Because not everyone is endowed with this ability in a natural way, it is something that you will need to practice on. There is a possibility that you are unable to plan things effectively or that you are unable to plan for the unexpected. However, if you take the time to think things through, you will be able to organize anything, from a straightforward barbecue to significant merger discussions with your manager. The trick is to get started on a small scale and gradually increase it.

You will be able to discover what you overlooked in your planning if you begin with a less ambitious plan (like that barbecue), which will allow you to make adjustments for the subsequent event. You will be able to achieve greater levels of success if you begin with something simple and work your way up to larger and more significant goals. Consider an experience that you've had in the past that made you nervous but ultimately turned out to be quite enjoyable. Have you ever been rock climbing on a mountain that was actually there? There is a good chance that you did not wake up one day and spontaneously decide to go climb a mountain. You probably worked up to it in order to get yourself ready for it. In addition to this, you should keep this in mind while you are planning new things. Do not rush into making that important presentation to the manager without first planning some of the more straightforward aspects of it.

It Is More Vital To Have Imagination Than To Have Information.

When Olympic coaches first began utilizing mental rehearsal and visualization techniques on athletes, scientists had not yet developed an understanding of the influence on the biological or neurological levels. According to recent research, having the same thought over and over again, particularly when accompanied by strong feelings that are chemically-related, can actually develop new neuropathways in the brain. These newly formed brain networks give rise to novel actions, and hence, results. It is also essential to keep in mind that the subconscious mind is unable to differentiate between imagined events and real memories, and that the hippocampus is able to store both types of examples. The brain and the body will show "evidence" as if an event actually took place if all that is done is mentally rehearse it beforehand. This is supported by the facts.

Because the subconscious mind processes information via images and feelings, the capacity to imagine is critical to one's success. Whatever you decide to write down as your Ideal Outcome for yourself, it needs to be more than just words. You'll want to use it to create a true picture, the kind of image that you can etch into your cortex and keep there until it turns into a memory (as far as your cortex is concerned).

Creating a mental movie is one of my favorite things to do since it allows you to combine your sensations and movement into the experience, which results in an increased sense of realism. You can start experimenting with this right away, but before you do, be sure that your "Ideal Outcome" has been given sufficient attention and has significance for you. It is essential to keep in mind that ten individuals with the same objective will come up with ten distinct pictures that represent their very own individual results.

Now, please take into consideration this next item because it is really important. You would still have something to work with and feed your subconscious mind if you only had your image and didn't construct a movie, but I want you to see what the movement and detail will do for you. Include as many specifics, sounds, and exciting elements as you possibly can. Do you remember when we discussed your five-sense self? You are, in a sense, going on a trip with that self (to the quantum field; however, you should not bring too much with you).

The mind is capable of remembering anything. When you go through the motions of seeing a movie in your head and then recollect the image that best symbolizes that movie at various points throughout the day, your mind is going to attribute all of the excitement and energy as if you were sitting there and watching the entire movie once more. Think of it like one of your favorite movies. All you need to do is listen to the theme music, and all of a sudden you'll remember everything that happened in the movie. This is somewhat analogous to that. You are going to create a moving mental movie, but you are also going to choose an image that represents the fact that your Ideal Outcome has already occurred.

Simply said, when we direct our mental and emotional energy toward a goal — one that we can "see" in our mind's eye — that image becomes inscribed upon the subconscious mind, as if it had already taken place. This creates the illusion that the desire has already been fulfilled. If this is the case, then your subconscious mind will present you with a wide variety of opportunities and ideas that will guide you toward the best course of action. This is not to argue that taking action on your dreams is not required; rather, what it means is that mentally rehearsing your Ideal Outcome will provide more opportunities and greater eagerness to take the inspired-by-intuition action that is necessary to attain them.

In addition to observing yourself in a scenario via the lens of a third person, it is crucial to put yourself physically into the action of the scene. This is something that Neville taught, but so few teachers actually understand it. For instance, you are not simply visualizing yourself admiring the pristine ocean while wearing your swimsuit and relishing your new position as "big boss." You are, in fact, currently resting on that beach, waiting for the adorable lifeguard to spread sunscreen on your stomach so that you can protect yourself from the sun. To put it another way, you are not closing your eyes when seated in the chair in your kitchen; rather, you are doing so while seated in a chair at the beach. It's difficult, I know, but that's why so few individuals are able to bring their desires into reality. Simply put some effort into it, and over time, it will become simpler to carry out.

Bringing Your Beliefs Into Line

Your vision board will assist you in concentrating more intently on the aspects of your life that you would like to change, but you must come to terms with the fact that it will require some mental exercise on your part to hush the terrified six-year-old version of yourself that lives inside of you. This version of you is the one that questions everything, does not trust the universe, and lacks faith in both yourself and the world around you. You may have the conscious belief that you are capable of obtaining success and acquiring riches, but if you continue to give permission to your subconscious negative thoughts to surface, you will sabotage your efforts to move forward on the path to earning success. You can count on making some blunders. Yes, you should be prepared for them, but the most important thing for you right now is to keep your focus on winning and achieving your goals. Don't forget to have patience with yourself throughout this process since it will take some time and work, and you'll need to be careful about the way you say to yourself when you experience any sense of failure or disappointment in yourself. Did you know that giving encouragement to houseplants by talking to them in a pleasant manner helps them grow better? Imagine the positive effects that might have on the mentality of a person...

Reducing One's Own Critical Internal Monologue

I noted before that doubts are negative, but when you want the Law of Attraction to operate, they are especially harmful.

You might be saying to yourself right now:

I am affluent.

Because I think and act like a rich person, I have no trouble attracting financial success.

When you want the Law of Attraction to operate in your favor, those are fantastic affirmations to say to yourself. But if you are also the type of person who quickly quits up at the first sign of difficulty or who may glance in the mirror and hear that inner voice telling you things like:

Who do you think you are kidding?

You will never achieve any level of success.

Don't bother wasting your time; there is no use.

Your mind is being trained to believe that you are not capable of achieving what you want to do, that you will not do what you want to do, and that you do not deserve to achieve the things that you want to do. If you unconsciously (and for some people, consciously) believe these notions, then the Universe will give you exactly what you think in accordance with those beliefs. If you are someone who experiences this on a daily basis and so frequently that it hinders your ability to take risks and commit to things, then elevating your frequency through changing the way you think could be the most important part of the manifestation process for you. Everyone has these negative ideas running through their minds from time to time, but if you are someone who experiences this on a daily basis and so frequently that it hinders your ability to take risks and commit to things, then you are someone who experiences this on a daily basis.

Because of the excuses they've made throughout their lives, many of the people I work with have let their goals languish on the back burner. Some of these explanations are really weak, and they will engender animosity in later years. Because of everything that has happened, you are further and further removed from the possibility of the Law of Attraction bringing anything great into your life. The way you view life is entirely up to you, and research has shown that an optimistic attitude far outperforms doubt and pessimism.

Maintain Your Unwavering Belief

Maintain your steadfastness in the face of challenging circumstances. It might be challenging to maintain one's faith when it appears that all possibilities have been exhausted. Never surrender your faith, no matter how difficult things get in life, no matter what. If you put your trust in God without depending on your own ability to comprehend things, he will guide you along the right road.

Our faith comes from God, who also brings it to completion. He is aware of the difficulties we face, and he is knowledgeable about the most effective means of rescuing us from those difficulties. Because you must believe that God exists and that he rewards those who earnestly seek him, it is impossible to please God if you do not have faith in either of these things. When you remain steadfast in your faith, God will bless you in ways that are far above anything you could ever hope for or imagine.

The following are five (5) ways to maintain a strong faith:

Pray without tiring or stopping.

However, faith is what actually opens the door. Prayer is the key. Never give up talking to God through prayer. Pray without doubt, keeping your thoughts and feelings uncluttered while you do so. When you pray, believe that the things you ask for will be answered in some way, and pray with faith. When you pray, God hears more than the words that come out of your mouth. He also listens to your heart, provides more answers than you ask for, and bestows upon you more blessings than you could possibly conceive.

Prayer is the cornerstone of achievement. Make praying a daily routine. Always make time to pray, and not just when things are tough for you but also when things are going well for you. If you don't pray, you leave yourself up to being hurt by the things that happen in life. Every obstacle in your life can be transformed into stepping stones for your advancement if you pray about it.

Treat other people with respect.

Always remember that everyone you come in contact with is going through a struggle that you have no idea about. You will be taken aback when you discover the extent to which someone is suffering on the inside. It's possible that you could be standing next to someone who is broken and depressed without having any idea of the struggles that they are going through. Learn to be good to others not because of who they are or what they could provide you, but because of who you are. Learn to be kind to people because of who you are.

Being charitable to other people has the power to transform not only yourself but also the wider world. The world is made a better place by people's random acts of generosity. No matter how insignificant the act of kindness you perform may be, it will never go to waste. When someone is going through a difficult moment, a little kindness can go a long way in their heart. The way in which you make other people feel about themselves reveals a great deal about who you are. As you assist those who are struggling, you will find that your faith is being strengthened.

Find your motivation.

When you're feeling down in the dumps, it can be helpful to think of other people whose faith has been miraculously manifested in their lives. Receive encouragement to assist you in remaining connected through your faith. Simply increasing your knowledge of those who have persevered in the face of adversity in order to achieve their goals can help to enhance your confidence in God.

Never surrender your faith, regardless of what difficulties may be thrown your way in life. Always keep in mind that the trials you face were not put in your path in order to bring about your demise. They have been sent to advance, bolster, and reinforce your position. If you can train yourself to maintain this mindset, you will never lose a battle.

Put yourself in the company of those who have strong faith.

Because you are only as good as the people you spend the most time with, it is in your best interest to increase the amount of time you spend with other people who are deeply committed to their faith. Your perspective will improve if you have meaningful interactions with folks whose faith is unshakeable. Attitudes filled with faith lead to deeds that are filled with faith.

If you want to be able to rise above the difficulties, troubles, and tests that life throws at you, it is imperative that you learn to maintain the proper religious attitudes. Maintain your unwavering conviction in God at all times, and you will never allow yourself to be overcome by your environment.

Recognize the positive qualities that you possess.

In order to make the transmission of your faith more effective, you must first acknowledge all positive that Christ has produced in you. Show your faith through action. Apply your religion in practical ways. Engage actively in the act of sharing your religion in order to gain a deeper comprehension of all the wonderful things that Christ has provided for you.

Maintain your steadfast faith. You are more than a victor, so live above hardships, difficulties, illnesses, diseases, aches, and anything else that brings you down in spirit because you are more than a conqueror. It is important that you not allow anything to cause you to lose confidence in God. Whatever it is that you are going through, it will not last forever, and if you maintain your faith and remain strong, you will emerge from this circumstance stronger and more capable than before.

Encouraged Behavior

You have a plan in place that will allow you to realize your objective or realize your ambition. This device operates continuously around the clock. This technique is effective, drawing to you whatever you require to make your idea come true. The servomechanism is the name given to this particular mechanism.

I have no doubt that you have ever sat down to see a movie about the conflict. A missile was launched in order to bring down a plane. Even though the airplane was making attempts to get away from the missile, the missile continued to pursue it. This is the servomechanism that is being used. Even if the target moves, the missile will still change its path to follow it and will continue to pursue it until it hits. The term "servomechanism" refers to the mechanism that is responsible for adjusting the trajectory of the missile so that it can continue to track the target. You have access to the same mechanism as well.

Your servomechanism is activated by a program that runs in your subconscious. As soon as the servomechanism kicks in, you will make a concerted effort to carry out the tasks that you have already drilled into your subconcious mind. The servomechanism draws to itself all that is essential to the operation of the subconscious programs successfully. Your subconscious mind will look for everything that is connected to your dreams and concentrate on finding it. Because of this, when you have a strong desire for anything, you will experience a number of coincidental occurrences.

In order for you to realize your desire, the servomechanism that is inside of you will go to work updating your thoughts, feelings, and behaviors. Servomechanism within you will attract the people, situations, chances, and coincidences as well as any resources you require in order to realize your dream.

Your own servomechanism will draw to you all that you require to make your dream come true. It's possible that this is both good and bad news. Because this technique is only effective once the goal has been reached. The Servomechanism does not care if the aim is beneficial to you or harmful to you as an individual. In addition to this, the results that you acquire will bolster the program that is running in your subconscious.

If you have put what we talked about earlier into practice, I believe that you have set in motion the servomechanism that will bring you the results you desire. At this point, all you need to do is go with the flow. If you take the time to look about you, you will most likely discover a number of fortunate coincidences and possibilities.

Concentrated Thoughts

You have a system that is referred to as the RAS (Reticular Activating System). Its purpose is to strip out the data that you have deemed to be irrelevant to your situation. If you try to organize the millions of thoughts that enter your head on a daily basis, you will go insane trying to do so.

Your mind is quite active right now, processing millions of pieces of information. However, they are filtered out by the brain, which does this by determining what you are focusing on. Take into account that what really matters is not what you want but what you focus on. The brain does not react to the desires and requirements of the body; rather, it simply reacts to what you think about and concentrate on.

Your brain will come up with even more reasons for you to despise your job if you keep dwelling on how much you detest it. People who are always griping will, as a result, continuously come up with new reasons to vent their frustrations. whereas those who are happy have an increased number of reasons to be joyful.

If you choose to get a red sports car, then you will start to notice that other people also drive red sports cars whenever you go anywhere. Are we just supposed to take them at their word? Absolutely not, because they are already present. What you see has been filtered by your RAS.

Recent events have seen me experiencing the same problem. I had been seeking for a specific book, and in the end, I was able to locate it by using an online store that sells old books. I decided to buy it. I was not familiar with the package delivery service, but I received proof that my product had been despatched through it. Their firm name is one that I had never heard of before. It kept running through my head. Then I looked up and noticed that their automobile had driven in front of me. In addition to that, I visited one of their workplaces. Have they just established a new office in my nation? Never in a million years. They were present from the very beginning of it all. Because of the way my RAS worked, I was never able to see them. But when I concentrated on it, my RAS steered my attention in that direction, and I was able to see it.

When you train your subconscious mind, you activate your servomechanism, and your RAS will guide your concentration to notice more possibilities, fortunate coincidences, and other forms of good fortune.

In his book "The Luck Factor: The Scientific Study of the Lucky Mind," Richard Wiseman outlines a research in which two groups of people, a "lucky" group and a "unlucky" group, were questioned about their perceptions of luck. They were given a newspaper and instructed to browse through it and tell him how many images were contained within it.

others who were fortunate were able to respond in a matter of seconds, while others who were less fortunate needed two minutes. The trick consisted of a huge statement on the second page that took up half of the page and stated, "Stop counting. In this newspaper, you'll find a total of 43 images. The fortunate group was the one that noticed it, whereas the unlucky group failed to notice it and continued counting.

Also at the same time, somewhere in the middle of the newspaper, on the pages of a large advertisement, was printed the line "Tell the experimenter you have seen this announcement, and you'll get a reward of $250." The unlucky bunch missed out on seeing it!

The unlucky group as well as the lucky group were both subjected to the identical occurrence. However, this is only true for a select few individuals. Being fortunate does not, in the end, have anything to do with being fortunate. It is only a matter of what you choose to concentrate on.

If you think you are a lucky person, you will attract more good fortune to yourself. There is no correlation between one's birth date, zodiac sign, or shio, among other things, and one's luck. If you tell your RAS that you are lucky, it will tell your eyes to look for further signs of good fortune. If you believe that you are successful, then you most certainly are successful.

Love Yourself First In Order To Maintain Your Calm.

The fifth stage toward instilling peace into your mind, body, and life is to cultivate a love for oneself through self-love practices. Self-love is defined as the ability to love and accept oneself. If you aren't content with who you are, it will be impossible for you to enjoy anything else about yourself or your life. You don't put much effort into grooming yourself, and as a result, your demeanor is becoming increasingly disagreeable. You are more likely to experience stress if you are becoming more unpleasant. Because loving yourself paves the way for acceptance and relaxation, you need to lavish affection on yourself and practice self-love if you want to become a true follower of manifestation through peace. This is because loving yourself paves the way for acceptance.

Methods for Cultivating Love for Oneself

First and foremost, in order to practice self-love, you need to be kind to yourself and acknowledge and embrace who you are. Get out your journal and write down everything about yourself that you dislike. Be as specific as possible. After you have expressed all that's on your mind, you should then take a pen and paper and write "I accept" in front of each of your shortcomings. About thrice each day, say to yourself around thirty times, "I accept myself completely and truly," and finish each session by giving yourself a hug. This will assist you in embracing your uniqueness, which will, in turn, assist you in gradually being more content with who you are.

Once you have reached the point where you are able to accept yourself, you will need to concentrate on overcoming your shortcomings and maximizing your strengths. Thirdly, in order to love yourself, you need to constantly thinking positively and prevent yourself from thinking negatively. This is because loving yourself is much easier when you think favorably about yourself.

Last but not least, you should make it a priority to identify your genuine circle of support and restrict your social interactions to people who are upbeat and supportive. You should try to limit the amount of time you spend with negative people, particularly those who are discouraging to you and who cause you to feel badly about yourself. According to a number of studies, increasing the amount of time we spend with upbeat and optimistic people has a beneficial effect on both our happiness and our stress levels.

You too may become pleased, joyful, and at peace with yourself by putting into practice some of these straightforward methods centered on the cultivation of self-love.

Take What You Can From Your Past Mistakes, Then Get Back Up Again.

You need to reverse the way you think about failure so that instead of viewing it as something that is so terrible and the end of our pursuits, you view it as something that can serve as an experience and an opportunity for you to learn. Pay special attention to the lessons that you may learn from your failures, and then use those lessons to propel you forward in your pursuit of achievement and financial success. You will be equipped with the ability to be resilient and confront future setbacks if you learn from your mistakes and reflect on them. Because giving up is the only way to experience failure, it should go without saying that if you do not give up, the word "failure" should not be in your language. Do not let the possibility of failing stop you from pursuing the thing that gives your life meaning.

Getting to where you want to go in life is never an easy ride. Along the path to accomplishing your objective, you will face a variety of difficulties and impediments. And it is necessary that you be mentally ready for these potential outcomes so that you are not sidetracked or overwhelmed to the point where you consider giving up. Do not surrender no matter how little or large a goal you have set for yourself; you must be ready for the fact that there will be times in the future when you will have to cope with difficult obstacles and even defeat.

For individuals who are on the path to success, having the mental fortitude to confront and prevail over obstacles that may appear along the way is the factor that determines whether they will be successful or not.

You begin by understanding and accepting the fact that there will be obstacles in your path toward achieving your goal. Therefore, before you begin your journey to achievement, mentally prepare yourself to face and triumph over whatever challenges you may encounter along the way. You should figure out a way to deal with and go through any obstacles that you encounter. You need to be able to learn how to encourage yourself despite the difficulties you face in order to reach your goals, despite the fact that working toward those goals might at times be really irritating.

The following are some strategies that can assist you in overcoming obstacles when making goals:

Determine any potential impediments.

When you first start out on the path to wealth creation, one of the things you should do is examine your goals in light of the potential obstacles you might run across along the way. It is not possible to anticipate everything that may occur. But there are numerous obstacles that you will be able to foresee if you take the time to carefully investigate the goals that you have chosen to pursue.

Identifying potential bottlenecks and outlining strategies for dealing with and overcoming them is an important element of effective goal setting planning. This is true despite the fact that we would prefer not to consider the possibility of such obstructions. You will be better able to devise a plan of action, which should include extinguishing any possible fires, if you anticipate and recognize potential problems. Create a list in advance of any potential obstacles that you may meet, and then devise a plan to cope with those obstacles based on the list. There are two types of obstacles: those that are internal to the individual, such as fear and self-doubt, and those that are external to the individual, such as a lack of money.

Be aware of the phenomenon known as the 'false hope syndrome.'

Setting a goal, being surprised by the amount of effort it required, and then giving up on achieving that goal is an example of what is known as the false hope syndrome. People are said to be suffering from false hope when they anticipate rapid outcomes but later discover that this is not going to be the case. When it comes to goal-setting, try not to get carried away. You should instead keep in mind that you need to be realistic and that there are goals that will demand you to define specific mini-goals and timetables in order to help you steer clear of having unreasonable expectations and to keep your attention on the task at hand. Keeping your momentum going might be made easier if you maintain your concentration by setting and celebrating the completion of a series of smaller goals.

Consider the difficulties you face to be learning opportunities.

It has been demonstrated that those who regard difficulties as opportunities for growth are more likely to have a positive opinion of their potential to achieve the objectives they have set for themselves. Do not beat yourself up over failures; instead, swiftly learn from the experience, and look forward to better times in the future. This will help you keep your emphasis on the good aspects of goal setting. It's not that successful people never have setbacks or that they face fewer hurdles than those who give up; the only difference is how those who walk out of obstacles positively see the circumstance. It's not that successful people never encounter setbacks or that they have fewer obstacles than those who give up.

It is not healthy to strive for perfection.

Your fixation with perfectionism might also serve as a distraction and make it difficult for you to concentrate. Do not subject oneself to standards that are impossible to accomplish, or you will be left with the impression that your objectives cannot be attained. Try not to put undue pressure on yourself. Have compassion on yourself, and don't forget to remind yourself that you, just like everyone else, are human and subject to the same kinds of struggles and blunders that we all experience.

Instead of focusing on the negative elements of mistakes, remind yourself that no matter how unpleasant, every setback is a learning experience. Positive thinking is good at helping individuals adapt and grow, so rather than focusing on the negative aspects of mistakes, remind yourself that every setback is a learning experience.

Keep your zeal alive.

Simply put, maintain your level of passion. Be careful to preserve the fire in your belly, both in terms of your drive and your enthusiasm, so that you can have the required focus on your objectives. In spite of the challenges that may be there, maintaining your focus on the achievement of your goals will be made easier if you often remind yourself of those goals.

Consider changing some of your objectives.

A simple review of your objectives is all that is necessary at times to keep you motivated and on the right path. It's possible that your goals need to be rethought in order to maintain your interest in them, to give them a fresh start, to incorporate new plans, or even to completely eliminate some of them.

Attitude is the key to maintaining focus over an extended period of time. If you have the appropriate mentality, you will be able to maintain mental focus during the process of goal-setting, which will increase the likelihood that you will be successful. The topic of how you can influence and cultivate the correct attitude within oneself is a simplified version of the subject of how you can remain focused and motivated to achieve your goals.

The ability to concentrate is critical for successful goal-setting and execution. You need steadfast dedication and constant inspiration to be able to achieve the goal that you have set for yourself in order to be able to maintain your concentration throughout the process of goal-setting. Because there is no easy method to reaching goals that will help us realize our purpose and vision, it takes consistent effort to turn a goal into an accomplishment, which in turn involves a persistent concentration on the task at hand. Having focus can allow you to materialize your objectives, making it much simpler for you to achieve them.

Maintaining your concentration and desire over the long term can be challenging, but doing so is absolutely necessary if you want to be successful in accomplishing your objectives. By putting these and other helpful hints into practice, you will not only be reminded of the significance of your objectives, but you will also be kept focused on achieving success and inspired to do so, all of which will contribute to the actualization of your vision.

In each attempt, you should prepare yourself to face obstacles and anticipate that you will encounter them. Roadblocks should not be the end of your road toward achieving your goals, nor should they be a reason for you to automatically deviate from the goals you have set for yourself. Investigate and figure out the reasons for the obstacle that you are currently facing. If it is something you can control, deal with it; if it is not, find a way around it that will not compel you to give up your dream. If it is something you cannot control, find a method around it that will.

Maintain your concentration by looking for fresh chances despite the challenges you are facing. You have probably already heard that some of the things that have been the most successful were never planned. Keep going by constantly reminding yourself of the victories you've already won; this will keep your spirits up and your resolve strong. You should use failures as motivation to work even harder to achieve the achievement you desire. Never give up the game.

For The Sake Of Holy Guardianship

This is one of the reasons why so many people choose to fast to God. According to the verse in Jeremiah 22:27, the Lord is the answer to all of our difficulties, and there is nothing that he is unable to accomplish."I am the LORD, the God of all mankind; is there anything that is insurmountable for me?"
Ezra 8:21 says, "then I proclaimed a fast there at the river of Ahava, so that we might humble ourselves before our God, to seek from Him the right way for us, our little ones, and all of our possessions." The fast was observed at the river of Ahava.

After spending time in prayer and fasting to seek God's face, Ezra was granted protection from God as well as direction from God. They prayed to God, and in response, God provided them with the answers to all of their difficulties. Because the thieves and robbers were waiting to steal all of their stuff, and because they required God's intervention, and because God gave them all that they needed for the protection, the proper things to do, the appropriate place to go, and the perfect means to hide their possessions from those that wish to steal them from them. He provided them with divine instructions and guidance that helped them find solutions to their issues, and as a result, their anxieties were dispelled. They deprived themselves of food and prayed to God for guidance before taking such a drastic measure. This is what the practice of fasting is capable of doing; it has a powerful way of pushing the heart of God towards assisting a person, and when this takes place, his hand, which is capable of doing all things, will be moved for the sake of that individual.

The whole fast for seven days, which entails taking water or juice but not any solid substance, is suited for this kind of situation; alternatively, one may embark on an absolute fast for three days, during which they do not consume any water or food in the hopes of receiving divine protection from bad and wicked people.

A VERSE FOR PRAYERS

O) You are my hiding place; you will keep me safe from harm, and you will encircle me with songs of salvation.... 7 of Psalm 32

PRAYER POINTS 1) Receive divine protection now in the great name of Jesus 2) Pray that the Lord would protect you and your loved ones from any and all forms of wicked agendas in the name of Jesus

3) In the name of Jesus Christ, His power will continue to be upon you so that you can triumph over any and all temptations.

Acquiring Expertise in Meditation

"Meditation is like going to the gym for your mind because it helps you build strong mental muscles like calmness and insight."

â€Ajahn Brahmâ€

When you meditate, it's like having a conversation with your spirit. It is possible to finish it before breakfast, saving you the money you would have spent on an expensive cup of coffee.

On the other hand, half of all Americans get it wrong. They give up after only one practice because they take the wrong strategy, and they don't even try again.

If this describes you, know that you are not to blame. Many of the programs currently available take outmoded concepts and attempt to use them in contemporary settings. There are as many different guides to meditation as there are treatments for hangovers. They are most likely all telling you to "focus on your breathing" and "clear your mind." But none of these things are required in any way.

The practice of meditation dates back to ancient times. When compared to how we ought to meditate now, the practice of meditating in the past was very different. In this day and age, we do not have the luxury of not having to worry about our children or of sneaking away from our community to meditate in a secluded cave. Because the way life was two thousand years ago is so drastically different from how it is today, we need to modify our approach when we meditate.

4 Suggestions to Help You Meditate

First Piece of Advice: Don't Stress About Emptying Your Mind

Trying to quiet your thoughts is like trying to get your heart to stop pounding. You are unable to complete the task. Except, of course, if you're already gone. However, one of the most widespread misconceptions regarding meditation is that it will empty your mind. It is OK for our minds to be busy all the time. The important thing is to give yourself some space and time to reflect, then redirect your attention to activities or ideas that help you feel more at ease.

Tip 2: Make Morning Meditation Part Of Your Routine

Your brainwaves will transition from a state of wakefulness to a state of restfulness as you continue to meditate. The normal condition of your brainwaves is one of relaxation when you first open your eyes in the morning. This indicates that you are already in a state that is conducive to meditation and that you should proceed.

Tip 3: Take Some Seats

Take a few moments to sit up and begin your meditation practice before you get out of bed and start getting ready for the day. If you want to avoid falling back asleep, you shouldn't lie down on your bed in a flat position. Make use of several pillows to support your upper body instead. Place your arms in a relaxed position on top of your thighs while you sit with your legs crossed. Then you should just close your eyes and unwind.

Fourth Piece of Advice: Put on Some Binaural Beats.

When you listen to music at two different frequencies at the same time, you may experience an auditory illusion known as a binaural beat. A frequency is played in the listener's right ear, while a different frequency is played in the listener's left ear. After that, the brain interprets all of these distinct tones and frequencies as a single tone. The use of binaural beats can enhance the power of specific brainwaves, making meditation and relaxing activities more effective. OmHarmonics, a program offered by Mindvalley, has a binaural beat with the name "The Deep Rest." It will take your mind from a state of rest to an active one, and then it will bring it back down to a condition of rest. It is a pattern that, if followed, will lead you into a magnificent state of meditation in just fifteen minutes.

The Meditation Process in 5 Easy Steps

Your thoughts can be organized and your self-awareness can be heightened through the practice of meditation, which is a guided activity.

Considered from a transcendental standpoint, meditation is best approached by viewing it as a discipline in and of itself. A practice of gratitude might be considered a transcendental activity. This is the place where you enhance your happiness vibrations by thinking on the good things that have happened in your life. One example of a transcendent practice would be to mentally picture yourself achieving your goals or to actively work on forgiving others.

The Five Step Meditation is a form of meditation that was derived from the work of Vishen Lakhiani, the founder of Mindvalley. It focuses on five different aspects of your life in which you should always be striving to improve.

Concern for others.
I am thankful.
The act of forgiving.
Your aspirations.
The day of your dreams.

The best part is that it will only take you ten to fifteen minutes, and then you will be well on your way to becoming your best self.

First and foremost, compassion

Being compassionate involves more than simply advocating for global tranquility. It involves having a real concern for the people around us and offering assistance to them when they are in a difficult situation. When you allow compassion into your life, you open the door for wonderful experiences and opportunities. You will have a more optimistic outlook, experience less stress in response to challenging circumstances, and it may even slow down the indications of aging. Not to mention the fact that compassion is the attribute that people covet the most in other people. Kindness and compassion are qualities that are universally seen as among the most attractive in a partner, regardless of gender.

During this stage of the process, you'll work on being a more loving person overall. In your thoughts, you will engage in the exercise of extending your feelings of compassion to everyone else in the room. Not only will the individuals you interact with on a daily basis profit significantly from this, but you will also find that it is to your own advantage. When you show compassion to others, you will find that it increases the amount of compassion you have for yourself.

How To Make Things Happen More Quickly

In the event that you are able to stick to this strategy, you will be putting yourself on the accelerated path to success! You are demonstrating something in a constant and persistent fashion! In point of fact, you are demonstrating everything in every single second. If this were not true, there would be nothing for you to experience; both your consciousness and the world around you would be a blank screen.

After all of that has been revealed, what evidence do you currently present for yourself?

The proper reaction is a straightforward one. You are demonstrating that whatever it is that you are concentrating on, you are aligning yourself with how you are feeling. If I had to guess, I'd say you're feeling better, getting healthier, and have a better handle on your cravings.

Or, to look at it from another angle, would you argue that you are concentrating your thoughts on the opposite? If you realize that your attention is focused on something that is counter to your craving, you will be able to see any reason why your craving is still absent from your existence and experience once you realize that your attention is focused on something that is counter to your craving.

To make a transformation like this, you must first fully acknowledge the way in which your awareness and the claims you make are the only "genuine reality" you have. The rawness of the world around you is merely an aftereffect of your awareness; it is not the reason for your awareness. Because you established the imaginative actuality firm in your mind initially, the reason for your physical symptoms just truly happens because of this. You have your creative mind and feeling state, and the purpose behind this is so that you can be able to immediately encounter the sign; the key to success here is to disregard your physical signs and appreciate the indication inside of yourself first. By doing so, you will allow your exterior reality to coordinate with this vibration, and you will also adjust to the experience that you are having.

The sensation of you waking up close to your spouse, your ideal automobile, house, work, and so on are out of nowhere and already existent; nevertheless, it has quite recently remained unperceivable to you due to the fact that you had not yet vibrated at the level which made it obvious yet. Convert this place and this moment into the vibrational match in order to open yourself up to the feeling of being physically present.

4

Your limiting convictions are the primary factor that will prevent or delay the appearance of your physical self since they will put a stop to all energy. Never believe that this is because "the other person isn't prepared at this point," you can't afford the vehicle, someone else has the activity you need, or the reality that you need is already here and ready for you to use! The exact opposite thing you should do when you are exhibiting is to originate from a position of need or need, or at the end of the day, need. When you do experience minor blips initially, relax and understand that you are supported by the universe. The exact opposite thing you need to do when you are showing is to originate from a position of need. You have to put your attention on that inner knowing that says, "if I can imagine myself with this ideal result, then it is now a reality for me," and you have to be absolutely confident that this is true.

Make The Decision To Put Your Happiness First.

As a matter of fact, the reason why it did not work for the majority of people is that "The Secret" did not place as much emphasis on the significance of having happy feelings as it should have. Affirmations and visualizing what you want in life are both useful tools, but they won't be effective unless you can also use them to tap into good emotions.

If you want to benefit from the law of attraction, you must first cultivate a more optimistic state of mind. Not only do your thoughts, but also the emotions you feel, have an effect on the world around you and the things that happen to you.

As a result, it is essential to enjoy one's self. It is essential to maintain a high level of positive energy, since this will enable you to become a magnet for all wonderful experiences.

Have positive feelings about oneself.

Having a positive attitude about oneself is one approach to improve one's mood and make the passage of time more enjoyable. You have to have the mentality that anything is possible and that you are deserving of love, happiness, and success in order to achieve such things. When you have a positive perception of oneself, you will experience increased self-assurance as well as increased levels of happiness.

Perform frequent physical activity.

Endorphins are a type of hormone that are produced in your body as a response to physical activity. Your mood will improve almost immediately if you maintain a regular exercise routine. You may go for a run, dance, or even give boxing a shot. In addition to this, you will experience more joy and a more stable sense of self as a result of your yoga practice.

Take in a good amount of water.

Your mood will likely worsen if you are dehydrated. Therefore, if you want to feel good, you need to make sure that you stay hydrated at all times.

Have some fun.

Make it a point to laugh at least once per day. Watching comedic videos on YouTube is all that is required of you if you are not feeling very well. Keep in mind that joy can also spread from one person to another. The simple act of laughing together with friends can go a very long way.

Take a break from the internet every so often.

The online community of social networking sites such as Facebook and Twitter is plagued by pointless conflict. If you want to be able to concentrate on the pleasant aspects of life, you need to disconnect from social media platforms like Facebook and Twitter for a while. Keep in mind that virtual reality cannot deliver the same level of happiness that may be attained through the genuine experience of actual things.

Put on your most impressive outfit.

Putting on your finest attire is an effective strategy for boosting your confidence and boosting your mood overall. When you take care of your appearance, you will notice an immediate boost in your mood.

Put an end to your habit of procrastinating and start working on the tasks you've been putting off.

You need to quit putting off your plans, whether it's in order to pay the bills or to find the person you will spend the rest of your life with. When you finally take action on something that you have been putting off for a long time, you will experience an immediate surge of positive emotions.

Give a call to someone you care about.

In the event that you are not feeling really well, all you need to do is give a loved one a call. You might give a call to one of your parents or to your partner. Talking to someone you care about and can put your trust in will quickly make you feel better.

Sing.

Singing in the shower is one of the quickest ways to feel better about yourself. It is okay if you are singing slightly off tune. To be honest, no one can even hear you.

Have a break from work.

It is essential to take a break from your strenuous labor and enjoy some time away from the office. Take some time off to relax and rejuvenate after the strain of the workweek.

Cheer up!

The nicest and least expensive item that anyone may wear is a happy expression on their face. Simply putting a smile on your face will immediately make you feel better about yourself.

You have got to learn to enjoy being patient. If the fulfillment of your wishes does not occur instantly, do not allow yourself to become disheartened. You need to have faith that the universe has wonderful things in store for you. Keep in mind that in order to feel joyful, you do not necessarily need to wait till you have what you desire. Choose to be happy every day because happiness is a decision you make.

It's highly possible that you are familiar with the concept. We'll talk about the law of attraction, but not the kind that relates to romantic partnerships; rather, we'll focus on the other version of the concept, which refers to an approach to personal growth that's gained a lot of support in recent years.

To think something like that, for instance, that luck will be on our side in our pursuits, is to have faith. You should want something with a great deal of zeal, optimism, and assurance, with the expectation that all of your long-awaited ambitions will eventually be accomplished. The well-known idea of the "law of attraction," which states that certain waves of energy articulate their influence for their own benefit, would be formed by these ideas, expressed in the simplest way possible. This theory states that certain waves of energy articulate their impact in order to benefit themselves.

This perspective conveys the message that "We are what we think." Vibrations that are capable of designing a mental state in which ideas are the reason and, as a result, the way to success are tuned and harmonized by us in order to bring about the creation of a mental state. Is there any way that could work? Is it reliable, in addition to that? It is worthwhile to discuss it in an objective manner given the significance it holds, particularly in relation to one's own growth.

The foundation of what we know as "the law of attraction"

The idea behind the 'law of attraction' has been around for quite some time. It is possible to trace its origins back to traditional theosophy as well as the "new age" movement. This theory has a "substrate" in the form of the field of energy and the invisible forces that weave the universe. Also, there is the concept of "positive thinking," which is a well-known and widely-promoted method for inspiring us and is able to infuse both energy and a sense of self-assurance in its recipients.

As a consequence of this, the so-called "law of attraction" can be understood in a wide variety of psychological contexts without any difficulty. There are a few of them that you might be familiar with:

The cognitive approach

A viewpoint that is excellent for the field of learning, in which cognition, or the many mental processes such as perception and memory, can assist in the process of obtaining new information and adapting to new circumstances.

Take, for example, the situation of people who are striving to give up smoking. Visualizing themselves beginning their days without that much-needed cigarette can help people make the transition away from smoking. According to the principle known as the law of attraction, our thoughts are the driving force behind our ability to realize our ambitions.

CBT stands for cognitive behavior therapy.

This psychological tendency is interesting because it teaches us that our thoughts cause our emotions and behaviors, which is a very important lesson to learn. Never use the phrase in reverse order.

To put it another way, it would be a method of exerting control over the emotional environment in order to put thought first. If I can convince myself to shake off my misery and remain resolute in my pursuit of that objective, then that idea will finally become the driving force behind my capacity to succeed.

Action is an alternative to relying on the law of attraction.

The only objective critique that can be leveled at the principle of attraction is that it places an excessive amount of emphasis on the realm of energies and the underlying concept that in order to acquire something, we must "ask for it." On the other hand, it is highly regarded when a person demonstrates thankfulness, positivity, and enthusiasm. Either the universe itself, or the presumably invisible force that both encompasses and binds us all together.

However, as we are well aware, merely posing the question is not sufficient. It is futile for us to demand those goals in our lives with humility if we are not willing to perform our share. Having a reasonable and logically consistent optimistic attitude is, of course, always appropriate and necessary. However, positivism must be maintained at all times. It is not sufficient to find solutions to our issues simply by thinking about them, wishing for them, or waiting.

Attraction and action are two sides of the same coin.

Let's embrace the idea that the law of attraction is the initial impetus for a change in perspective, which entails thinking about what it is I desire, acknowledging that there are things about myself that I need to improve, and making a concerted effort to achieve my goals. As a direct consequence of this, the "law of action" needs to be included. Once you have your eyes and your hopes open, it is time to start the engine of transformation.

Those who instill a sense of pride in us for the things we have achieved. You can't count on the energies to work on their own to give you what you want. Don't put your faith in them. Establish your means, your tactics, and your path forward on a daily basis, and keep in mind that your efforts are the driving force behind every success.

The principle of attraction is an effective means of generating drive. However, keeping in mind the fact that the "concept of positive thinking" currently sells many self-help books, it is always a good idea to look at things in an objective manner.

Changes That Can Be Made

As was discussed earlier, there are three stages involved in living an intentional life. You are going to want to examine each one, and then you are going to want to take them one at a time. If you believe that you are capable of doing all three of them at the same time, you are free to choose whatever option is most convenient for you. But you shouldn't let the adjustments you're making completely take over your life just yet. If you are experiencing feelings of being overpowered, you should take a step back, calm down, and remind yourself that you are working toward becoming a different person—the person you are supposed to be, rather than the person you have been.

When you first start out on your path, you need to make sure that you ask yourself some pertinent questions. What do you want to achieve by directing your life toward specific goals? In what specific ways are you willing to alter the situation? In what ways do you anticipate those adjustments being implemented? And how will the decisions you make influence you and the people you care about, both favorably and negatively?

Check in with yourself and see if you're receiving what you want out of life. Are you making progress toward your objectives? Do you even bother to set any goals for yourself? After giving yourself and your life a thorough examination in the mirror, you have to make the decision for yourself as to whether you are living for the sake of others or for the sake of yourself. It is not inherently a terrible thing to be living for other people, but if you are doing it without concern for the influence it will have on your own life, then you will not find genuine happiness as a result of it. In point of fact, you are setting yourself up for a life of misery if you do not take into account your own pleasure and achievement.

The following are the steps that you are required to take:

Maintain control of your thoughts by accepting responsibility for them, and examine both the inside and the outside of your head when assessing your personal reality.

Gain an understanding of who you are and the motivations behind your actions. Examine your experiences to develop your own unique perspective.

Act on what has to be done, make smart choices, and keep your motivation up.

First, a Look at Your Present Situation
To have a clear picture of what has to be changed, you must have a comprehensive awareness of your current situation. You will take into account the various aspects of your external environment, such as your social circle, your place of employment, your house and family, and anything else that is going on around you that has the potential to divert your attention away from your own pleasure and advancement.

In addition to this, the atmosphere you have within yourself is also very essential. This would include any patterns of thinking, behavior, or emotions that you have that you find yourself fighting against on a daily basis. This indicates that you will feel anxiety, anger, pain, and hurt as a result of the situation. And by living intentionally, you will know how to work through these setbacks to put your hope and faith in your mission, what you were genuinely created for. This is because you will have learned how to work through them.

During this time of review, you are likely to be influenced both positively and negatively by other individuals. Some people could look down on you because of the changes you've made. You will come to understand who your true friends are and who is not, as well as who will stand by you and who will not. If you want to have a happy and successful life, you might find that you need to make some significant life adjustments, even if these are not always simple choices to make. This necessitates getting rid of certain individuals in your life, switching careers, or signing up for a fitness club membership in order to shed some pounds and get in better shape. You cannot count on everyone's support, but the people who are already on your side are the ones you know you can rely on. Maintain contact with them. You will never outgrow the desire for good friends.

The second step is to gain a personal insight.

When you have taken the time to examine your life, you will arrive to a profound comprehension of both yourself and the people around you. Not only the people that are now in your life, but also other people. You will have a better understanding of the available possibilities. Not only will you have an understanding of why you do the things that you do, but you will also have an understanding of why other people do the things that they do. When you have knowledge like this, it will be much simpler for you to deal with situations in which you feel insulted or betrayed. It is possible that you will not feel any better after doing so. However, you will comprehend the reasons behind why that someone is acting in the manner that they are.

You should not turn down the opportunity to gain a profound grasp of human nature, especially your own nature. This is a vital quality that will help you calculate the options that are accessible to you and assess how well each of those roads will help you achieve success and happiness in your life. If you possess this trait, you will discover that it is easier to attain success and happiness in your life. Your subsequent move will lead you along the most advantageous road, which will be to your advantage in the long run.

Step Three: Accomplishing What You Set Out to Do
You have reached the moment where you will start taking action and putting your decisions into action. Now is the moment to start your quest in earnest. This is the time in which you will work

on achieving your goals, removing the negative from your life, and bringing the positive into it. You won't be able to prepare yourself for the challenges you'll face. It's possible that you'll have to stand up to the harmful actions of other people who want to hold you back and keep you from moving forward.

You have the chance right now to let go of those detrimental things and focus on developing the positive behaviors instead. You will need to adjust your course as you move forward if an opportunity presents itself that takes you in a different route or if an obstacle forces you to travel in a different direction. Your objectives ought to be adaptable enough to be in line with what it is that you are capable of achieving. You are going to be the one who makes the adjustments, and your dedication to the job is going to be the factor that determines whether or not they are successful. Do not place an unnecessary amount of strain on yourself by striving to achieve something that is clearly beyond your capabilities. This might include things like the curing of an illness, regaining the ability to walk after having been paralyzed, or the prevention of blindness or deafness.

You may start living more consciously and improve your life by making choices and decisions that are grounded in realism.

Creating A Spot For Parking Vehicles

The books become new friends who have been absent for a long time, and what better way to begin than to uncover mysteries? Who wouldn't want to know the "secret" to achieving their goals and living the life of their dreams? At some point in their lives, most people will probably give some consideration to the idea of realizing their goals and objectives in life.

However, the question that needs to be answered is whether or not it is possible to attain success by following the same procedures or process for many years and expecting different results.

The response was, still is, and will forever be a resounding no.

As a result, I made the decision to put my scientific mind to rest and simply comply with the coach's instructions for the following thirty days. The coach suggested building daily reading habits as a means of bringing about change in one's life.

Since I already had a PhD and had passed the National Eligibility Test, you could argue that I was through with my studies or reading at that point. Despite the fact that I have always read advertisements. My mind was forced into a state of sabotage, procrastination, prejudice, and pessimism as a result of excessive reading of the scientific paper, all the worldly responsibilities, and just the twists and turns of the past. Reading was no longer something that interested me since I had come to the conclusion that it didn't lead anywhere, despite the fact that I had a PhD and more than a decade of professional experience.

However, the class completely shifted how I thought about reading in general.

Reading anything that does not inspire or motivate you in any manner will not in any way open doors or doors for you. However, the reading that results in triggering those neurons in your brain, those hormones in your blood, and those twinkles in your eyes will undoubtedly alter the course of your life.

I began reading "The Secrete" after the coach had led me into complete darkness. The bedrock of the coaching profession and the essential building blocks for achieving one's goals. Even though I had the book in my possession for around five to six years and had even read a few s from it, I did not feel anything when I read it at that time. It's possible that I was too preoccupied with my misery to notice.

However, in accordance with what the guide advised, "just follow," I made it a habit to read ten pages from the book first thing in the morning. The first seven days of the book failed to pique my interest in any way. Things were like this for the second week, simply read it. You need to read it. The third week was when things started to get magical, and by the fourth week I couldn't get enough of the book; it quickly became the one I would most strongly suggest to anyone. I was inspired to take action by the book, which described how the author started the voyage of manifestation by manifesting parking space. I made the decision to put the universe to the test. The author described how he consistently manifested a parking place with a success rate of 95%, and how the remaining 5% of the time he only received a space when someone else pulled out of the spot.

I was on a mission to test the cosmos while engaged in a conflict between my scientific mind and my manifesting mind.

I made the decision to bring about the materialization of a parking spot in my preferred location within the office complex. I always discovered that the site was occupied, and I realized that today was going to present a significant obstacle for me. Before leaving my house, I expressed interest in reserving this parking spot; let's examine the extent to which such arrangements are feasible. And you won't believe this, but the parking lot was as full as it normally is. My constantly racing thoughts told me that nothing was going to happen, and I continued on with a sense of disillusionment in my heart.

But here's where things get surprising: right away, a thought popped into my head that the author also said how approximately 5 percent of the time he received the parking place when someone else took out their vehicle. My mind flashed on this idea immediately. After having that notion, I looked over to my favorite spot and knocked on someone who appeared to be getting ready to exit their vehicle.

And ever since that day, I have the ability to constantly manifest parking space, even in the busiest parts of town or the arenas that are completely full.

The lesson I took away from that day was that although my win was in the 5 percent bracket, it was still a win. The universe emerged victorious, the tools and strategies we were being instructed in were successful, and, last but not least, the book itself was producing the desired results.

On that particular day, though, I had the epiphany that the most important action I could take toward realizing my ideal life was taking the first step. It was really straightforward in terms of planning and establishing the objective. I was able to get the exact location I wanted to park in since I had carefully planned it out in my head before I started driving. And finally, and this is the most important part, I took a baby step toward fulfilling my want and building my faith so that I can fulfill even greater desires.

I came to the realization that a lot of us are making the error of expecting the great wishes to get manifested within a short period of time without having rock-solid confidence in the universe. This is a mistake because a lack of faith allows fears and doubts to sneak in, which finally leaves us with a feeling that we have failed. Every one of us is connected to the energy of desperation. I was attempting to make a significant change in my life without a firm grasp on either universal faith, precise planning, or baby stages. The result of which was that I was left with a horrible sensation, a sense of hopelessness, and the ability to switch into auto-pilot mode.

Throughout the course, I was changing my routines, practicing thankfulness on a daily basis, beginning with audio recordings of affirmations, shifting my mentality, learning new things—even if they were very simple—but carrying out everything I was instructed to do.

The practical guide to attracting and manifesting loving relationships is covered in 6 of the book.

You can genuinely use the law of manifestation and the power of your subconscious to attract love and amazing relationships, even if you haven't found "Mr. Right" or "Ms. Right" yet. If you are still looking for a partner, this applies to you. The following is a list of some of the steps that you can do to bring love into your life:

Begin with a blank sheet of paper — If you have previously been in a relationship that was tumultuous, codependent, or abusive, there is a good probability that you have already developed a pessimistic outlook on romantic partnerships. You have to get rid of all of the emotional baggage from your previous relationships in order to attract and manifest the romantic partnership that you have always dreamed of having. You have to get rid of the emotions of fear, doubt, cynicism, anger, and regret in order to go forward. If you genuinely want to move on with your life and have satisfying relationships with others, you will need to let go of these feelings.

Develop a romantic relationship with the person who holds the most significance in your life—you. First and foremost, if you want to attract a loving partner into your life, you need to love yourself. One of the most significant relationships you will ever have is the one you have with yourself; it is of the utmost importance. You are required to pay attention to and respect your own feelings and emotions. You need to get rid of the negative influences in your life. You are required to take into account your personal preferences and needs. You are responsible for the health of both your body and your mind. Consuming nutritious foods and maintaining a regular exercise routine are essential acts of self-love. You must also practice self-compassion and make every effort to steer clear of activities, circumstances, and occurrences that could be considered stressful. Do things that bring you joy on a regular basis. Take part in pursuits that bring out the best in you. Pursue activities that spark your interest and excitement. It is much simpler to bring love into the world when one first learns to love and accept oneself without conditions.

Put your desires for the future of your relationship in writing and be as clear as possible. Be truthful and sincere with yourself. In addition to this, make a list of the qualities that you hope your future mate will possess.

This is just one illustration. Roshelle, a lady in her late thirties, is still holding out hope that she would eventually find someone to share her life with. She wrote down the kind of relationship that she wants to have, as well as all of the qualities that she wants in a partner, and she put both of these things down on paper. She jotted down "tall, funny, dark-hair, a businessman or a professional, intelligent, responsible, honest, trustworthy, fit, handsome, and sporty." After working for the same company for a short while, she decided to seek new employment and relocate to a different office. There, she made the acquaintance of a man by the name of Christopher who had all of the characteristics that she has listed. They decided to get married after a period of six months and are currently enjoying a happy marriage.

When you are more explicit in your request, the world responds to you more rapidly.

Imagine and make room in your life for your potential future spouse. Close your eyes at the end of each day and picture yourself with your significant other. Become aware of all the beneficial vibes. Get a good feeling. In addition to this, make room for your potential future spouse. Make your life and the life of your potential partner more compatible with one another by arranging things in such a way that it will be simpler for them to incorporate themselves into your life. Invest in a bed with a double size, clean out some space in your closet, and remove all the clutter from your home.

Believe in yourself and have faith. You must have faith that you are deserving of love and that it is on its way to you. You have to think that it is possible for you to have this particular relationship and to have that particular person in order to bring into existence the kind of love that you are looking for.

Have a good time, and don't let the time pass you by! Enjoy every moment of your life and make the most of the time you have to wait. The secret is to make sure that you are having a good time and spending a significant amount of time ensuring that you are taking advantage of every opportunity to do so. Go engage in some mountain climbing. Attend a course that focuses on your personal growth. You should start your own company. Visit some stores. Move around. Donate your time. Follow your interests and pursue the activities that excite you. In this manner, you will have a lot of information to impart to your companion.

Techniques Of Manifestation Utilizing Reiki

Manifestation is a tactic that can be utilized to achieve a variety of goals, including getting a job you love, switching careers, buying the car or home of your dreams, meeting the partner of your dreams, amassing wealth, developing influential connections, curing an illness, and other similar accomplishments. There is no limit to what you are capable of manifesting; but, you are need to engage in the appropriate approach in order to accomplish so. There are a few different approaches that are being used for appearance, the most well-known of which are the power of your intuitive nature and Reiki. In the realm of psychic force, there are a variety of approaches, such as contemplation, insistence, seeding and representation, and so on; nevertheless, the procedure in Reiki is significantly simpler. However, in order to do so, you will need to make use of

Reiki pictures, which can be learned as part of the Reiki Second and Third Degrees (Level-2 and Level-3A), respectively. However, there are some educators who do not even broach the subject of manifestation, even though some teachers make it a significant part of their lessons. After displaying each of the four photos, I move on to Level 3A and demonstrate same method there.

The practice of Reiki is commonly thought of as a method for curing primarily physical conditions, despite the fact that this is not actually the case. There is a significantly wider range of applications for Reiki than just that. One can make improvements in nearly all aspect of their life by utilizing Reiki, including the manifestation of a particular goal or intention. You are only able to manifest one item at a time, even if you are familiar with techniques such as the law of attraction and the use of brain power. However, if you are familiar with these techniques, you can use them to manifest. On the other hand,

Reiki can be used to simultaneously bring about the manifestation of a number of different goals. When you begin the manifestation process, the all-inclusive strengths begin to develop and transform the conditions driving the realization of your purpose. This needs a major investment of time and energy. It could take a few days, weeks, or even months depending on what it is that you are trying to bring into existence. Targeting more difficult goals will undoubtedly take more time. Not only this, but a considerable amount of it also depends on how correctly you are employing the technologies. You need to maintain a consistent work ethic and show tolerance. If you allow yourself to become overly excited, you will end up wasting your energy. Worrying over things does more harm than good. You are free to ask for anything. That being said, there are certain morals that one ought to follow, despite the fact that there are no restrictions on it.

If you are looking for a good job, for instance, asking for a position that somebody else is already filling is inappropriate since you are inadvertently demanding the termination of that other person, which is out of line. Take a uniform approach to managing the various issues.

When looking for someone to share one's existence with, this is also the case. Make every effort not to ask for a particular person. That might happen despite your best efforts. Make your needs known regarding the characteristics that should be present in your partner. Your ideal companion will be brought to you by nature.

When asking questions, use common sense. It is best not to ask for a house on the moon because doing so is not feasible.

Never, ever, ever intend to cause harm to another person since, in addition to the fact that your plan won't be successful, you also run the risk of injuring yourself in the process. Remember the age-old proverb that "What you send, returns to you" (what you give, comes back to you).

to maintain a simple existence with fewer needs and desires while demonstrating an increased capacity for giving.

If it is not too much trouble, please appreciate the gift that has been offered. Continue living your life without complaining about it to other people at any point. Acquire the favors, and then make an effort to build on them. Awesome will assist you in achieving all of your goals and gaining all of your distinctions. We engage in arduous activities with the eventual goal of becoming more capable. So just keep living your life as best you can and keep going forward with what you've been given. Daily appreciation is an important part of the Reiki practice. Believe that Reiki is always there to protect you and provide you with things that are for your highest good. Reiki will always be there.

Liberation From Contemplations Of The Negative

This is going to cause a significant vibrational shift in you. It's time to rethink how you relate to your negative ideas. This time, it's permanent.

It's time to quit berating yourself for having negative thoughts and start loving yourself. Be kind to yourself and do things that make you happy.

There are a lot of people in the community of manifestation and the Law of Attraction who are afraid of the following: "I'm into positivism and the Law of Attraction. My thoughts shape the world I experience. Oh my goodness, I keep having terrible thoughts, and now I'm terrified that they'll become a reality. It makes me sad. Despite the fact that I've been studying all of those upbeat items, I still have negative thoughts. I am unable to make any progress. At this point, my greatest concern is that I will become preoccupied with my own anxious ideas and worries.

It's high time we stopped making excuses! To begin, even the most upbeat and optimistic individuals have moments where they find themselves thinking negatively. And just because you are having a bad thought does not guarantee that it will immediately materialize into a problem.

Do you recall what was discussed in the before this one? Imagine that you had entertained the idea of having a suitcase stuffed with one million dollars lying on the table in your kitchen. And the effects can be seen right away. At the same time, visions of a thief breaking into your home and robbing you run through your head. He is literally standing at your front door, ready to rob you.

To our good fortune, things don't turn out that way...

Naturally, we are not granting you permission to entertain unfavorable ideas in any way, shape, or form. Maintain awareness and continually examine your train of thought. However, you should be aware that they do not hold any power over you, and that it is not the case that they will automatically materialize into something dreadful.

Make a commitment to yourself that you will not punish yourself for having unpleasant thoughts. Simply having negative thoughts is already bad for your health and welfare as a whole. They block you from moving on and keep you living in fear. The vast majority of people are ignorant of spiritual and mental rules; as a result, whenever they entertain any contrary notions, they simply continue to dwell in those thoughts. Their negative thoughts act as a sort of internal GPS that may direct individuals to locations that they would rather avoid. We're talking about undesirable signs and symptoms here.

Thankfully, we don't see the results of our negative ideas right away. in order to provide you with the space and time necessary to make the transition to a more positive mindset.

Be thankful, too, for the fact that your mind sometimes brings you unfavorable thoughts in order to keep you safe. And it's possible that having some negative thoughts can be helpful. For instance, you may find yourself having unfavorable thoughts about the possibility that your trip or vacation will be postponed. Consequently, you could make the decision to safeguard yourself by purchasing sufficient travel insurance.

This is an illustration of a positive example of a bad mindset that leads to specific preventative activities. We are of the opinion that the practical and the metaphysical should be combined. Therefore, a person who is having unfavorable thoughts about their impending trip could decide to alter their travel plans, switch their airline, or purchase the insurance that will provide them with greater tranquility. At the same moment, people might make the decision to affirm, "I am safe, I am guided, I am protected, God, angels, and the Universe take care of me."

The golden rule is to be careful without becoming anxious about it.

But you shouldn't make the conscious decision to focus on the negative. You are an endless creature, and you have the ability to change the way you think about things at any time. Ask yourself, "Can I allow myself to think about the things that I love?" alternatively, "Is there something positive that I can allow myself to look forward to?"

Repeat the following affirmation: "Right now, I am safe and protected."

Simply put, it's accurate. When you let your mind wander too far into the past and the future, you give it the opportunity to develop negative thoughts and feelings. It's like going through time, but without any of the benefits for you. It's time to just flat-out refuse!

But you shouldn't be too hard on yourself since we can show you a fast shortcut to the manifestation of your desires that will immediately bring you greater happiness and tranquility in your mind.

You have to realize that your focus should be here and now, in the now. Simply being is all that is required of you. Sense the calm and security that surrounds it. Treasure this time. Take a few breaths in and out deeply. Coming and going.

Direct your complete concentration toward your heart. Literally, give yourself permission to let go of your thinking and concentrate on your heart instead.

Do you feel like all the bad energy is melting away?

Your heart serves as your internal compass. It is the highest level of consciousness you possess. Allow it to steer you.

When you are faced with a challenge that needs to be overcome, rather of focusing all of your mental energy on finding a solution as quickly as possible, take some time to enter your heart and focus on how you feel about the situation. Accept the benefits of mindfulness. Always keep in mind that you are strengthening your ability to materialize things by bringing your awareness into the center. Your practice of manifesting will go to the next level as a result of this exercise. It will assist you in becoming more at peace, thoughtful, creative, and productive in your daily life.

We are well aware that there may be some matters that require your urgent attention, and that you may not always have the opportunity, the time, or the space to enter your heart. In certain circumstances, prompt action on your part may be required.

But, truly, the more you give yourself over to the here and now, the fewer unfavorable circumstances you will attract into your life. Because of this, with time, you will finally be able to enter your heart more and more.

This strategy strikes dread into the hearts of many individuals because they cannot bear the thought of surrendering control. Even Elena have this trait.

However, I want you to know that you can continue to fulfill your daily commitments and tend to your employment as you normally would. Simply said, you should remind yourself to take a few brief breaks multiple times during the day in order to regain your composure. Your current reality will begin to change rapidly as a direct result of this fresh, serene, and aware energy. It will seem like magic when it happens.

Please give this a thorough reading more than once, and don't dismiss it just because it's straightforward. This is the missing piece in the manifestation puzzle for a lot of people! Who could say? It's possible the same thing will happen to you!

Keep in mind that you are in a secure position at the time. You have absolutely nothing to be concerned about. You should have faith in yourself. You are not bound by what has happened in the past. And the future is being shaped right now to accommodate your needs and ambitions.

You are on this earth to have happy experiences, and as such, you should share the happiness you feel with other people. You have been set free. Your history no longer holds any sway or influence over you.

Incorporate that joy into your very being by recognizing the significance of the here and now. Take the preceding exercise as well as this very carefully. It will completely transform your life. The only thing you need to do is put in some practice.

When you wake up, make a connection with your heart. You are not required to get out of bed at this time. Remind yourself that you are protected, cherished, and cared for in the best possible way. You are living in this moment, and this is your reality. Instead of beating yourself up for having a negative idea, you could have a conversation with yourself in which you ask, "Oh, isn't that interesting? It serves as a gentle nudge to consciously transform myself into something that is more empowering!

And whenever you find yourself going through any unfavorable "what if" scenarios, simply reframe them as good "what if" possibilities.

For instance, a question like "What if I apply for a new job but won't get it?" might be reframed as "What if I apply for a new job and learn something new and discover a new method of doing job interviews?" or "What if I apply for a new job, get accepted, and double my salary?" respectively.

People are heard to express their frustration by saying things like, "Oh, I can't visualize, I can't affirm..."

However, humans constantly engage in visualizing and affirming. It's only that people who aren't conscious of spiritual laws keep confirming and envisioning things that focus on the negative, and they don't even realize it.

Now, the moment has come to move on to something that is more empowering. Act out the scenario as if it were a game. Start working out your spirit by heading to the gym. Yes, you will most likely skip some days, and some of the days you do complete might be cheat days. Forgive yourself and focus on making the best possible progress moving forward.

mostly due to the fact that the power of the present moment is constantly waiting for you. And when you do connect to it, all of the negative energy from the past disappears. It's settled. Left no trace.

And last but not least, here is a piece of advice from Elena. She doesn't do much more than repeat the mantra, "Only my positive thoughts manifest." Because you now have the knowledge that we passed on to you through her in this , you are immune to the damaging effects of negativity.

And if you want to take it a step further, you may reinforce and embody your new truth by saying things like, "Only my positive thoughts manifest."

You have no limits whatsoever. You have a lot of power. You are unstoppable by whatever means. You are allowed to be who you are and to pursue the things that make you happy.

Because you are in the world. Simply said, because you are. And because you have the awareness that unfavorable thoughts do not have any influence over you. They are merely a sign to assist you in shifting into a more positive mindset; however, this time you will achieve even more success!

from the past disappears, it's seeded belief no trace.

And I'met but not least, here is a piece of advice from Elena. She doesn't do much more than repeat the mantra, "Only my positive thoughts manifest". Because you now have the knowledge that we passed on to you through her in this, you are immune to the damaging effects of negativity.

And if you want to take it a step further, you may reinforce and embody your new truth by saying things like "Only my positive thoughts manifest".

You have no limits whatsoever. You have a lot of power. You are unstoppable by whatever means. You are allowed to be who you are and to pursue the things that make you happy.

Because you are in the world, simply said, because you are. And because you have the awareness that unfavorable thoughts do not have any influence over you. They are merely a sign to assist you in shifting into a more positive mindset, however, this time you will achieve even more success.

170

www.ingramcontent.com/pod-product-compliance
Lightning Source LLC
Chambersburg PA
CBHW011958090526
44590CB00023B/3767